TEXTILE PALETTE

Creative Fabric Painting for All Skill Levels

Kelsey Samuel

Table of Contents

CHAPTER ONE

INTRODUCTION

Ceaselessly rules to Paint on Surface Brilliant sight on surfaces and various materials is focal and sensible. You might have looked at an old shirt or something else with an expressive plan and thought about whether you could give it new life by adding your imaginative spunk to it. This could appear, clearly, to be a perilous specialty persistently, yet this illuminating movement will tell you the drifter bits of the best philosophy for painting on surface, the right contraptions, and the materials expected to make a stunning painted piece, as well as unambiguous tips and cheats to make a keen strategy of hand-painted articles of clothing or complex plan things. Choosing the Right Surface When choosing a method for painting a surface, it's best to have complete control over the material you use so you can choose the right paint for your project. Painting garments, cushions, shoes, upholstery, and surfaces are a colossal piece of the time cleaned by crafters and specialists that could right as of now have a thing at the chief spot of the need list that they mean to illuminate and deaden. Assuming you mean to obtain new surfaces, you will likewise be supporting surface affiliations.

THE KIND OF SURFACE YOU COULD PAINT ON

Surface is assuredly not your all around common surface to paint on. Surface strands and surfaces shift as per the material substance and quality. It is truly imperative for do all major evaluation going before bobbing into hand-painted pieces of clothing or things, particularly continuing through you are new to the craftsmanship. You'll start to acquaint requests like how with paint denim and whether acrylic paint tumbles off garments. In any case, you can really paint on most surfaces; Strength and adaptability are unquestionable characteristics shared by all of them.

Standard Surfaces Silk, fleece, cotton, and surface are splendid choices for painting surfaces. Colors normally dry unequivocally, save well, and are prosperous in assortment paying little heed to what the way that paints can spread and drench the external layer of the material. Standard surfaces will work strikingly with most kinds of paint. Paints will relatively set best with standard filaments over facilitated strands.

Surfaces Made of Organized Materials a huge piece of surfaces made of created materials, similar to material, nylon, polyester, and denim, have had their strands inaccurately treated to safeguard them. When applied to the material's external layer, these phony materials likely won't match your paints well. It is ceaselessly stayed aware of to pre-wash these things to dispose of these coordinated substances, which will get the paint a long way from sticking to the outside layer of the surface. Because of its flexibility to paints, denim is a great decision.

Which paints can be used to paint surfaces?

Paints don't all work commendably on a great many things. Paints can make your things look astonishing, yet picking the right materials at first is basic. The best paint type can be picked once you have your leaned toward surface. Surface paints and groupings, acrylic paints, shades, and inks, as well as various paints, are the best paints to use while sorting out a decent way to deal with paint on a surface, truly.

SURFACE PAINT AND PLANS

Surface paint and ink are the best choices for painting things and dress. These mediums will stick very well with most materials. Surface paints and assortments perpetually change the substance obligation of the materials' strands without changing the surface. Surface paints are best for hand-painted clothing and other items, while colors require a significant amount of paste to adhere and are best for projects that cover more prominent surfaces with more obvious surface locations. Colors are also great for displaying things like sprinkle tone. Surface paint and shades are launder able, adaptable, and don't inundate surfaces.

The best paint for painting surface is: ZENACOLOR Surface Paint for Pieces of clothing Set

The ZENACOLOR Surface Paint for Garments Set is an extraordinary choice for youths to talented surface painters and crafters. There are 14 clear tones here, including metallic and standard shades. The surface is matte, the paint dries rapidly, endures perpetually, and These paints are truly unpretentious in any occasion be made thicker with an additional gel medium. Crafters seeking an efficient method for painting on clothing will find these options to be incomprehensible.

Acrylic Paint; could acrylic at whatever point anytime paint be applied to surface? Basically, the reaction is "yes!" Acrylic paints blend well in with cotton and denim surfaces.

How should acrylic paint be taken off from dress?

They are customary, astoundingly strong, adaptable, and easy to utilize, and open in different varieties. The significant issue with acrylic paints is that accepting an over the top proportion of paint is applied to the surface's external layer, they will break. Purchase a surface medium to mix with your acrylics to aid in the paint's setting and adhesion to the surface is maintained. Defeating you decided to work with acrylics for surface convincing craftsmanship on Shirts or different things, being have some knowledge of this past placing all that into making your last framework is head.

Best Acrylic Paint for Painting Surface: U.S Workmanship SUPPLY STORE 25 Blend Set of Preposterous Acrylic Paint

This acrylic paint set from U.S Workmanship SUPPLY STORE is a reasonable choice for crafters needing to make eye-getting and impacting mix expects surface. There is no need for a surface or gel medium, and the groups blend well together. These paints cover a huge surface region and dry rapidly. Regardless, lighter shades could require additional layers of paint.

Tones and Inks; most of tones and inks used to paint clothing depend on liquor. These mediums have a more unnoticeable area of joining and are inclined to spill and soak the strands. In the event that tones and inks are utilized decisively, they can make an impressive, watery impact across the outer layer of the surface. Similarly, working with tones and inks can very challenge. They are not sprinkled as every now and again as surface paint, so they might become cloudy after some time.

THE SMALLTONGUE: An energetic and successful surface printing ink is Surface Screen Printing Ink. It works with various tones, including genuine manager tones. They are incredibly useful for stenciling and the second nuances of hand-painted dress. The utilization of a power weapon or setting the paint after your diamond has dried is proposed thinking about how these inks are not exactly dependable.

Various Sorts of Paint

Most of paints are colorfast and viable with surfaces. You can work directly or close by incalculable mediums the choices are unending. You could consolidate liquids for block painting and silk screening, sprinkle paints for stenciling, and markers for line work, fine detail, and text making. You could likewise use paints to cover more significant surface locales and upholstery.

The Qualities of Surface Paint

Acrylic Paint, and Inks regardless of the way that sorting out a possible strategy for painting on surface can be a truly readiness cycle, knowing your paints and how their characteristics could impact depending upon the sort of paint you pick is a pivotal greatness. A critical partner that pushes toward the moving qualities of surface paint and collections, acrylic paint, and tones and inks is right away.

CHAPTER TWO

HOW TO SET UP YOUR SURFACE

Before beginning your creative plan, you should make several designs for your surface in order to paint the most striking piece of clothing or fashion item. After selecting your surface, evaluate how it will perform in conjunction with paint mediums.

Pre-wash your Surface

On the off chance that you've chosen to paint a model on a piece of clothing you at this point own or gotten, you ought to ceaselessly pre-wash it! Washing anything, old or new, will help them with returning to their uncommon size and discard any overabundance starches and made materials in the materials. Pre-washing basically permits the surface to get back to its last size and work better when paints are applied. Your things should be washed in a garment washer at a low temperature or the most potential troublesome way.

Iron Your Thing

The surface you pick will affect this push toward general. Two normal sorts of surfaces, cotton and material, have a penchant to turn out to be more unbending and wrinkle. To streamline made by workmanship process, it is upheld to run an iron over the surface until it is level. Denim-like materials are resistant to wrinkling, so smashing these thicker surfaces is unnecessary.

Fix Your Material to a Barrier

If you want to paint clothes with multiple layers, such as T-shirts, it is best to put a barrier between the layers to prevent paint from seeping in and adhering to them. To safely adhere the texture to the board, you can use a hardboard or cardboard box along with a few bulldog clasps or washing stakes.

Prior to painting garments or different things, hose the texture

Prior to painting your plan, you can apply a meager fog of water to the texture's surface. This will inconceivably chip away at the restricting of the surface with paint. Be careful of the consistency of water application and don't include an abundance of water the grounds that the surface could develop and wind as it dries.

BIT BY BIT DIRECTIONS TO PAINT ON DENIM DIRECT ADVANCES

In this educational activity, we cover the fundamentals of painting dresses forever with acrylic paint. These phases will guide you towards making your striking arrangement on a denim coat. At the point when you have aggregated your devices and materials, you can fire setting up your workspace and in a little while sort out some way to paint on surface! An enormous piece of the instruments and materials expected for painting articles of clothing and things will be speedily open inside your home, or studio space. The accompanying instruments and supplies can be utilized to set up your work area once you have your favored paints available.

1. Your choice of surface

2. Hardboard or cardboard impediment

3. Bulldog fastens or washing stakes

4. Give bottle water

6. Faint pencil (2B or 3B)

7. Compass

8. Paintbrushes

9. Water holder

10. Acrylic paints, surface paints, inks, markers

11. Clothing iron or hairdryer

Step One: Ensure Your Work area Is Ready With Every one of the Devices and Materials You Should Figure out How to Paint Denim. Set up the Texture. Also, make sure the fabric has been pre-washed to get rid of any starches and synthetics that might be present. Iron the surface gave that key. At the point when the denim is fixed to the block board with bulldog cuts, place it near your organized arrangement.

Step Two: Hose the External layer of the Surface

Gently and dependably shower two or three layers of water over the area where you expect to paint your arrangement. Keep the splashes reliable and try not to apply an excessive amount of fluid to the texture's surface on the grounds that doing so could make your artwork be mutilated.

Step Three: Pencil: Sketch Your Arranged Plan With a dull pencil, sketches your organized plan. This should be an incredibly key format of what you plan to make, the better nuances and assortments will come through when you begin adding layers of paint. Share during the time spent orchestrating across the surface and make it a highlight let your own touch and style shimmer.

Step Four: Paint Your Organized Arrangement

Begin painting your organized arrangement with your picked materials. The craftsman utilizes markers and acrylic paint in this instructional exercise. Start by painting your experiences first, and then keep painting the front until you've captured all of the little details. At the point when you are happy with your painting you can clear and clean up your workspace.

Step Five: Permit to Dry while it is as yet joined to the hindrance board, permit your painted texture to dry for something like 24 hours. While it is drying, this will prevent it from smearing or bending. At the point when it is thoroughly dry, you can kill it from the limit board and put it on a holder.

Step Six: Set the Paint with an Iron

Turn your garment back to front. To set the paint, iron the underside of the painting on medium to low heat. This will guarantee that the paint will not fade or break when exposed to sunlight. To set the paint forever, you can likewise utilize a hair dryer or intensity firearm a couple inches away from the denim.

TIPS AND BEGUILES FOR SURFACE COMPOSITION

While finding and attempting various things with how to paint on articles of clothing in the means above, there are an unprecedented few clues and misdirects that can help with your cycle. The following are a couple of thoughts for you, whether you're new to the craftsmanship or have done a couple of tasks with texture painting previously.

Guidelines to Wipe out Unfortunate Mistakes While Painting Pieces of clothing;

If you have committed a blunder some spot in the beginning stages of your creation, you can wipe out unfortunate engravings and mix-ups simply by using color and a paintbrush over the area you wish to erase. Before removing larger areas of your paint for garments, it is recommended that you test the interaction first. You can moreover use whiten to have charming effects on hazier materials.

VARIOUS SYSTEMS FOR SORTING OUT SOME WAY TO PAINT ON ARTICLES OF CLOTHING

There are with everything taken into accounted various strategies and effects you can make on surfaces. If you don't plan to make clothes that are hand-painted, you can use stencils instead. You can attempt various things with many procedures and styles. Additionally, you are strongly encouraged to combine your materials and mediums. Weaving, strips, dots, gems, and, surprisingly, extra textures can be generally added to your painted plan. You can truly zero in on your painted surfaces essentially by hand washing them in lukewarm water and allowing them to air dry. This holds the paint back from chipping constantly and obscuring in the power of a garments washer or dryer. Exactly when you are air-drying your surface, make sure to keep it out of direct light as it could really hurt serious sun the artistic work. You can now make a beeline for your closet or the nearest secondhand store to find your next item with these fundamental steps and advice on how to paint texture properly. Tweaking your pieces of clothing with surface paint and embellishments will give your thing a completely unique life and put a little kick in your step. Showing something particularly yours while remembering the climate will encourage you.

BASIC TEXTURE PAINTING TIPS FOR YOUNGSTERS

At one point in time, I was focused on Surface painting. I had to draw some plan or theme on everything I sewn. I could have made much better fabric paintings on napkins, aprons, and bed sheets if I had read this post earlier. No usage crying over unenlightened posts, which weren't even made back then. Different kinds of supplies you can buy for better texture painting You can start painting your texture with three basic colors red, blue, and yellow and a few brushes. In any case, despite the fact that your significant other's eyes begin to move with each new buy and your pantry is spilling over with make supplies with no space for even another brush, it is consistently good to realize that you can purchase more.

Brushes

1. Round tip brushes - You can buy a minute round tip brush which is ideal for making little nuances, and a more noteworthy round tip brush

2. Level tip brushes, furthermore called Shade brushes - These turn out ideal for disguising and highlighting. You can moreover include this brush for blending.

3. Liner brushes - As the name suggests, lines are drawn with these brushes.

4. Frothing Apparatuses - You can use these brushes in case you have an enormous district to be covered. These foam brushes go with a wooden handle.

5. Paint-filled outliners are planned explicitly for making three-layered frames, which are important while performing fluid weaving on pieces of clothing.

6. For sure, even Permanent markers for a quick masterpiece gadget - phenomenal for structures and dull drawings.

Upgrades with Photoshop, plunge pens, stamps, wipes, or another retentive utensil, can be all around used appropriately. Choose a soft brush for watercolor washes and effects.

CHAPTER THREE

ORGANIZED STAMPS, STENCILS, OR PLANS AND MOVING MATERIALS

For inspiration for surface composition plans, Checkout this post on 10 inspirations for winding around plans; they turn out ideal for surface canvas moreover.

Paint

What paint to use for surface artistic creation?

You should preferably be using Acrylic surface paint/material paint; they contain a variety suspended in an acrylic medium exceptionally made arrangements for use on surface.

Notwithstanding, you can similarly use commonly helpful acrylic paint for hand painting on material, gave you mix surface medium to make it sensible for painting on surface. A surface medium is a thick fluid that looks hazy when wet anyway dries boring. Normal Acrylic paint dries hard on the surface and may break after it dries, but the medium makes it more malleable/versatile. The medium is mixed in a degree of 1 area surface medium to 2 segments acrylic paint. Mix totally and use.

Acrylic texture paint can likewise be utilized with the texture medium.

It is used to debilitate acrylic surface paint without changing the shade of the paint. If you use the medium to debilitate acrylic paint instead of water there is less biting the dust?

Utilize medium in a 5:1 proportion with the paint to accomplish a watercolor impact with acrylic paint. On the off chance that you could do without the lustrous look, there is a Matte Medium that can be added to acrylic paint to make a dull matte impact. If you plan to splash paint, you can add a special medium that gives the paint a spray able consistency and prevents the sprayer from getting blocked. Texture paint is regularly blended in with puffy medium in a 3:1 proportion. For example, mix one drop of texture paint with three drops of puffy medium. Simple paints are ideal for a variety of texture painting techniques like splash bottle impacts, salt impacts, stenciling, batik, and splatter techniques. They are also light and clear, allowing fundamental tones to appear on the other side. They capability as a fluid color when joined with water in a 1:1 proportion, and a few brands could in fact be utilized to color ties. You by and large use these assortments on light-shaded surfaces.

HOW TO INCLUDE ASSORTMENTS IN SURFACE ARTWORK?

Red, blue, and yellow the essential tones can be joined with high contrast to deliver a great many shades. Nevertheless, having a couple tones convenient is perfect. A piece of the assortments you could have to buy in case you are needing to paint on surface an extraordinary arrangement Dull Red, Ultramarine blue , Yellow ochre, Indian red, Consumed sienna, Rough sienna, Unrefined Umber and Madder brown, cerulean blue, and Cobalt blue , then, at that point, the reliably significant high differentiation. You can give your feline a few shimmer and aspect by shading it in pearlescent or metallic shades. Glowing/Pearlescent Shading Medium can be added to standard paints to add shine.

Which is the best surface for surface artistic creation?

A light tinted 100% cotton surface with a somewhat close weave is the most sensible for painting with surface paint. This is why I enjoy painting on cotton bed sheets so much. It is very fulfilling, as I would like to think, to buy plain bed sheets and afterward change them into a masterpiece. Great cotton shirts act as a brilliant starting point for texture painting. You shouldn't, however, restrict your texture painting to cotton. You can have a go at painting on various types of surfaces like silk, silk, rayon, cotton/poly blend, sewing surface, fleece, material, material, silk organza, calfskin, terry material, velvet, extravagant, cowhide, and most designed surfaces; offer your expertise a chance scarves, furniture, shirts, tunics, window hangings, cushions, and embroideries in different sorts of surfaces. In case you are painting extensive brush strokes with gigantic arrangement districts it is gotten a kick out of the chance to work with a free weave surface (Vaguely woven surface allows a more prominent measure of the assortment to penetrate the fibers), but for little nuances and versatile plans, an all the more close wind of the surface is major..

Surface paint is applied to the external layer of the surface; in this manner, a slight thickening of the area is undeniable. You will see this on lightweight surface like muslin than on heavier surface like material and duck texture.

THE BEST TECHNIQUE TO PAINT ON CONCEALED SURFACE

Right when you paint on the concealed texture, the issue is that the assortments will look obscured - you ought to add many layers for it to focus on some degree undeniable. One straightforward method is to paint a layer of white inside the plan and then, when it is completely dry, dry the plan however you like. Because of this, it will be more obvious. Subsequently, for this present circumstance, you will require a lot of white paint - if the arrangement is gigantic.

1. A couple of holders with clean water

2. Material/tissues to wipe and dry brushes

3. Plastic sheet to protect your surface from staining

4. A Styrofoam sheet/cardboard sheet covered in plastic which is barely more noteworthy than your arrangement (to be put under the painting district so that paint wouldn't stain the contrary side of dress.)

5. A plastic range for joining colors Gel Medium (discretionary) Gel medium can confer a polished or matte completion to

the paint or they got done with painting. It can give a very strong, water-safe, UV-safe, non-yellowing cautious covering for your surface work of art.

An alternate iron this could have all the earmarks of being expected after you move paint from an actually finished the most common way of painting dare to your daughter's white school uniform without a doubt, that is the very thing I did.

GUIDELINES TO DO SURFACE WORK OF ART PHYSICALLY - LITTLE BY LITTLE

Step 1: Prewash the surface

This is an essential step, especially for garments that you will wash. You ought to dispose of the estimating/surface finishes applied to the surface in its gathering cycle. Differently, the paint won't cover all fibers, and when you wash the painted surface, the paint could break off and show openings where paint should be. Subsequently, prewashing is generally best. However, don't worry about prewashing when painting on textile-covered furniture, sacks, or accessories that you won't wash. Accepting you are painting an old piece of clothing, guarantee it is immaculate and it is without starch or conditioner. Iron the locale where you are thinking about painting. Wrinkles will bend the surface and hence crafted by workmanship.

Step 2: Set up the workspace

You should in a perfect world start managing a level surface covered with plastic. Paint won't leave this kind of stain on your worktop or floor. Stretch the surface adequately and keep it on an ideal safe place where it can stay undisturbed till it is dry. The best is to keep it on a sheet of thick cardboard sheet covered with waxed paper, so the paint wouldn't release and make a disaster area under; Moreover, the waxed paper guarantees that the paint won't stick. It can basically be cleaned off later and used later. In case you are painting inside a shirt, keep a plain thick paper or plastic piece inside. A paper would get the job done. This will hold paint back from staining the back. Make a Styrofoam screen that you can extend the texture on assuming that you find that you paint a ton; this can be connected with pins, resulting in a texture that is fairly long and wrinkle-free. While painting, some people use cooler paper to avoid the possibility of settling the texture. A cooler paper more prominent than the arrangement is joined plastic side down on some inadmissible side of the surface. Iron from the top. This will stick the cooler paper on the surface and you will have a momentarily solidified surface with next to no wrinkles permitted to be painted. Simply remove the cooler paper once the artistic creation is finished. Surface paint and acrylic paint harden when it is in contact with air so keep the compartments shut while not being utilized; take similarly as much relying upon the circumstance onto the reach. For each tone, utilize various brushes, and never dunk your brush into paint that is as of now in the jug. You will crush the whole compartment.

Step 3: Types of texture painting

You can freehand draw your plan on the texture or use one of the exchange strategies shown to move the plans. Start painting by putting paint on the brush. It is more intelligent to include one single brush for one tone with the objective that you don't have tangled assortment. Draw the outline first and subsequently starting from the outwards to inside fill the arrangement. Use firm short strokes to fill.

Different techniques for surface composition

Surface canvas ought to be conceivable exactly the same way that you paint on material; to create an aspect, layers upon layers. Additionally, texture paint can be used in a variety of ways to produce a delightful painted effect on texture.

1. Sprinkle salt to have a magnificent popped effect.

2. Apply relaxed wax with a brush and subsequently apply paint on the surface. Paint will enter through the breaks of the wax and result in a batik print on the surface.

3. Stenciling: The most well known technique for painting texture is stenciling. Using a cutting tool, you can cut out the inside of a printout of your favorite picture to accurately paint on it.

4. Stepping; Paint is applied to a stamp that has been cut into the ideal shape. Check out the post on how to make simple stencils at home. This is then placed on the surface. This is a most cherished system. You can work on surface stamps. To make texture stamps, follow the instructional exercise. Then again the informative activity to make potato stamps

5. Wet surface before painting for a watercolor influence. Simply soaking the fabric in water before painting suffices.

6. Splash painting.

7. Marbling is the cycle by which the shades of the paint are drifted on an uncommonly pre-arranged shower in

whirls and different examples. When the fabric is placed on this bath, the paint looks like marble.

8. Splatter paint

9. Sun Painting, this incorporates using a layout/cyanotype surface and different things to lay out associations. You can endeavor this strategy using your reliably painted surface and found objects like leaves. You will discover a negative print of the found object imprinted on your fabric if you allow the painting and the found object to dry together. In the post on Outline texture/cyanotype texture, find out about blue printing. Always use less paint on the brush than you think you need when painting. Haziness can be

expanded, however paint force can't be diminished except if you paint over many its has dried.

THE BEST WAY TO CONCEAL WITH TEXTURE PAINT

Most of the guidelines for acrylic painting you achieve on material work with surface like you paint faint assortments first and a while later layer lighter tones on top. You paint the establishment first and subsequently the nuances. Anyway by then, there are no set perpetually leads are planned to be broken. Layering and concealing with texture paint can be done in two ways. One is to conceal after the primary layer of paint has dried (since the paint is long-lasting when dry, painting over the primary layer will not cause it to fall off) and the other is to mix dark and light tones while the paint is still wet on the texture. Paint can dry extremely quickly on the brush, making it difficult to work with or remove; keep it soaked continually.

Step 4: Assortment mixing

Assortment mixing is wizardry. You will be flabbergasted at the extent of assortments you get by mixing two or three essential tones in moving degrees. Red and Blue and Yellow are the fundamental tones. Additional tones are produced when you combine them in various ways into one. Exactly when discretionary assortments are mixed you get a whole scope of tertiary tones. So you can start with the fundamental tones and do all the fine art you want. Yellow and blue can be combined to produce green, and red and blue can be combined to produce violet. Orange is made of red and yellow. Violet, green and orange are the discretionary assortments. A mixing of the Fundamental and Discretionary assortments outfits us with the last level Known as Tertiary Tones. On the variety wheel, reciprocal tones are the ones that are inverse each other. Check the red rose and the green forgets about to see that God clearly understood his integral tones. The ideal tones for combining should be these. You should consolidate dark or hazier essential tones to accomplish more obscure shades. Any tone can be made lighter by adding white to it. A pastel shade is achieved by adding white. Expecting that you really want direct filling, add water to the paint. To accomplish uniform inclusion, you might have to layer on numerous occasions. You can get a gritty hued tone if you join all of the fundamental tones as one. Change the assortments, and you get different shades of brown. Add dim to this, you get a more dark brown. Green tone is one which you will find you will use again and again if you love bloom plans as I do. Take Yellow and add little bits of green till you get the shade of green you want. Combine some blue with lemon yellow for a pure green. Add a couple of red bits to the yellow and blue combination for an olive green tint. For a more dark shade of green you ought to start with a hazier shade of blue.

Bit by bit guidelines to add a layered shift center over to your surface work of art

Expecting that you use one single assortment on a thing, the picture will look level and one-layered. Normally, there will be times when you favor that appearance. In any case, if you need to apply a three-layered shift focus to an image, remember to add three tones of the same color. The image will appear to be nearly real if you mix a light shade, a medium shade, and a dim shade and keep them hidden. Clearly, contingent upon how you mix and shade it.

Keep in mind that acrylic paint and textile paint leave permanent strokes, so you can't experiment and hope they wash off. It cannot. If you find your mistake rapidly enough you could have the choice to scratch off the paint expeditiously with a reach edge, yet don't depend on it.

Step 5: Hold on

Keep it together for 24 hours before you wear it or wash it or iron it. Verify that it isn't adhering to anything.

Step 6: Heat set Following 24 hours; the artistic creation should be warmed to become long-lasting. The methodology for setting the texture paint will be framed on the mark. It regularly prepares you to push on the opposite side of the work. You can warm set the front of the plan with a squeezing material or material paper for security notwithstanding the rear of the work for good grip. Use as high-temperature setting on your iron whatever amount of the surface can persevere, and press without steam, for 30 to 45 seconds. Now and again you can warm set solely on the veneer of the arrangement like because of an upholstery cover on decorations; You must make use of press material. Do whatever it takes not to use steam. In addition, never do it directly on the painted surface at whatever point you iron it. Think about how conceivable it is that you have a surface which you would rather not press (like cowhide or completed surface) then, a fundamental hair dryer can be used to dry the paint .You ought to apply it for close to 30 minutes for it to totally fix the paint. To warm puffy paint, hold a heated iron at a distance from it. This way the puffiness will not fix (like it would if you iron from the back) If you have colossal painted surface that you get no opportunity to warm set with squeezing and crushing, use a dryer - the power in the dryer could set the paint. Apply heat on every single piece of painted surface, guaranteeing that all area of the arrangement connect with the force.

Step 7: Washing the painted thing. You shouldn't wash the painted thing for something like 5 days - that is the base time it will take for the paint to totally fix. Turn the garment back to front while washing. I recommend hand washing the painting or using a gentle cycle and mild detergent if you want it to last. Spill dry instead of machine dry for the imaginative creation to persevere.

CHAPTER FOUR

DIRECTIONS TO CHANGE ACRYLIC PAINT INTO SURFACE PAINT

I don't figure making custom Shirts will anytime become unfashionable in the causing situation. There are so many enjoyable activities. What's more, a short time later add to that various inspirations to change surface, weaving, sewing, sack making, even Halloween troupes, and there are around a million purposes for surface paint in the causing situation. Moreover, tragically, due to reasons I will not at any point grasp, surface paint is both really exorbitant, and it generally comes it little containers. Why?

Furthermore, why do a lot of surface paints simply have a little execute tip like the dated "puffy paint" we used in the 90's? Am I developing myself? It's ordered "layered surface paint" by and by which decidedly sounds extensively more intricate, ha. Regardless, I'm here to tell you that there's not precisely a need to purchase a totally new plan of arrangements on the off chance that you truly want to do some surface work of art. Notwithstanding the thing surface you're painting, you can sort out some way to change acrylic paint into surface paint rapidly for significantly less money and with boundless assortment decisions.

What is surface paint?

Surface paint is a sort of acrylic paint that is unequivocally made arrangements for use on surface. It has more versatility than various kinds of paint so the surface won't feel firm after it's painted. Additionally, it has been designed to allow the texture to be washed and worn. Surface paint is most often used to assortment little to medium size areas of assortment. On the off chance that you wanted to assortment greater locales or an entire piece of surface, surface tone may be the really fitting choice.

Why might it be smart for me to change acrylic paint into surface paint?

1. Texture paint is commonly more costly than acrylic create paint.

2. Acrylic paint is available in more shades than texture paint, giving you more options.

3. There could currently be a ton of acrylic paint in your home.

4. Similar end result regardless. It's agreeable to investigate.

Painting Fabric: Some Hints and Tips Wash and dry your fabric in the same way you would normally before beginning.

1. Do whatever it takes not to use purifying specialist.

2. Iron your texture to make a work of art surface that is smooth and flaw free.

3. Shield your work surface as paint would leak through.

4. Expecting that you are painting something with more than one layer like a Shirt, put something between the layers (tinfoil, cooler paper, cardboard, etc) to keep the paint away from leaking through.

5. Sketch plans with an evaporating ink surface pen before you start painting.

6. Couldn't care less about your coverall or painting garments.

7. Accepting you are mixing tones, work up more than you normally suspect you will require so you don't run out.

8. Right when the paint is dry, set the surface paint according to the rules on the things you've used.

BIT BY BIT GUIDELINES TO CHANGE ACRYLIC PAINT INTO SURFACE PAINT

The most un-requesting technique for changing acrylic paint into surface paint is by adding surface medium or material medium.

What is material medium? Material medium is a liquid that you mix in with acrylic paint that allows the paint to be more thin, every one of the more sensitive and versatile and very sturdy on surfaces. Nowadays a lot of acrylic paint associations make their own material or surface medium to add to their paints. I have endeavored the Delta version and the Liquitex and they're awesome, but FolkArt and various associations make it now also!

BIT BY BIT GUIDELINES TO MIX ACRYLIC PAINT AND MATERIAL MEDIUM

Follow the headings on your material or surface medium whatever amount of the time, you simply mix identical bits of your acrylic make paint and the surface medium. Blend well and it's just as simple as that! There has never been a simpler way to do this. I like to mix my acrylic paint and surface medium together in a little holder with a cover like a kid food compartment. Like that, I can save the surface paint for later if I want to include it for another endeavor then again expecting my surface paint dries and I truly need to add another coat or last detail any locales. On the off chance that you have blended a custom tone, this tip is particularly useful. If your new surface paint really gives off an impression of being fairly thick, you can add a bit more surface medium. Then again in light of the fact that both of these things are water based, you can a dab of water to thin the surface paint. Then, at that point, apply paint to your ideal, dry, squeezed surface (recollect that step that we analyzed in the tips and misdirects portion) with a brush, a q-tip, a foam brush or another standard masterpiece gadget that you like.

What measure of time does surface paint expect to dry?

Surface paint dries fairly quick, just to some degree more delayed than ordinary acrylic make paint. In any case, most material mediums will have a particular proportion of time that they recommend permitting your errand to sit before you set it as well as wash it, to allow the paint to totally fix. Try to scrutinize the characteristic of the thing you use for those rules.

HOW YOU MIGHT SET SURFACE PAINT

On the material medium you use, follow the dry time and setting headings. Most often this incorporates permitting the paint to sit for quite a while (habitually 48-72 hours) and a short time later "setting" the paint with a dry iron, being sure to cover the painted locale with a pressing texture to shield both the paint and your iron. From that point forward, you can for the most part commend not surprisingly.

How could texture paint be tidied up?

Cleanup with cleaning agent and water a lot of like normal acrylic paint. Piece of cake. However, just like acrylic paint, texture paint won't come off of your clothing. Wear a dress in this way!

The accompanying request I will get presented is:

Could acrylic at any point paint be changed over into texture paint without the utilization of texture medium? This is an extraordinary request and I have a possibly questionable reaction. Permit me to start by inquisitive with regards to whether you have anytime gotten acrylic paint on your pieces of clothing and you didn't see until it dried? Then, have you at any point endeavored to eliminate it? It's basically tremendous, right? If you are painting something where you can't muster the energy to care accepting the painted section is in general very fragile and versatile, you can absolutely paint on surface with straight acrylic make paint. I would do this for a Halloween outfit that will likely just be worn once and won't be washed on numerous occasions. Several surface shoes would be brilliant as well. This could also be used for more creative things like layering paint on top of texture in a montage or mixed media project. Then, utilize that acrylic paint on your texture with no guarantees. I wouldn't use acrylic paint without surface medium on anything that you really want to gift, keep, wear on and on or wash again and again. The surface medium is basic to make the thing solid and pleasant to wear or contact.

By what other method could texture at any point paint be produced using acrylic paint?

As per what I've perused on the web, you can utilize family supplies to make texture paint out of acrylic paint in two extra ways. Permit me to begin by saying that, despite all advice to the contrary, I truly enjoy providing you with tricks and tips that I know work. I have not tried either of these methods, so continue.

The glycerin procedure:

This method incorporates making your own material medium by going along with one area white vinegar, one segment vegetable glycerin and two areas water together. That amounts to half water, 25% glycerin, and 25% vinegar. That makes a handmade "surface medium". Then, as shown earlier, you combine that with your acrylic paint in proportions. Heat set with a crushing material and a dry iron when it is dry.

Why employ this tactic? To be sure, expecting you at this point have those trimmings at home it could save you cash. Then again you presumably will not have the choice to find material medium where you dwell. Then again you might just have to dissect?

The strategy utilizing paste and shaving cream:

This procedure makes a thicker surface paint that is a trick for "layered paint" or "puffy paint". Mix 3 Tablespoons of shaving cream in with 1 Tablespoon of standard school stick. From that point forward, variety with acrylic creates paint. Apply to the texture in the manner you need, and give it somewhere around 24 hours to totally dry. Heat set with a pressing material and dry iron.

Why use this procedure? Children would have loads of tomfoolery taking part in this one. As reliably defend your work surfaces and guarantee they are head to toe peddled in coveralls?

THE END

Made in the USA
Columbia, SC
20 December 2024

50166832R00043